Queen of the Limberlost:

The Gene Stratton-Porter Story
(as told by her animal friends)

Written and Illustrated by Meg Ellen Grandfield

This book is dedicated to my brood, Jessica, Amanda, and Andrew.

-M.E.G.

"The Queen is here!
It is our friend, Gene!"
chirrups Andrew Robin.

Jessica Blue Jay calls,
"Jay! Jay!
She is as beautiful
as the dawn!"

Mandi Duckling quacks,
"Quack! Quack!
She is our guardian
from trouble!"

Olivia and Oliver Owl hoot,
"But let's start at the
beginning!
On August 16, 1863, a
light shines in the
Limberlost cabin nusery,
showing a cooing baby,
Geneva Grace Stratton."

Carrie Lou Cardinal chirrups to her mate, "Baby Gene plays with us in the pasture while her family plows the fields!"

Helen Hummingbird hums,
"Father teaches Gene to whisper
near our nest, so we love her visits!"

Hilda Hen cackles, "When Mother explains that Reddy Rooster's crows will cause the last egg to stop hatching, she is cccccorrrrect!"

"Gene loves us! She nurses us if we're injured, and we become her pets,"chime Hezikiah, the blue jay, Bobbie, the bantam hen, and Hank, the red-tailed hawk.

All of nature sings a chorus,
"Father proclaims
that she is
Queen of the Limberlost
Swamp!"

Mr. Blue, the heron, squawks, "Gene loves nature in the spring, summer, fall, and winter!"

Danny Duckling quacks, "Gene and Laddie have lots of fun playing Keep-Away with us in the stream between their farm and our farm!"

The moth flutters, "Gene loves to read her father's books in his library....

...and paints her winged friends, the birds, moths, and butterflies for her books!"

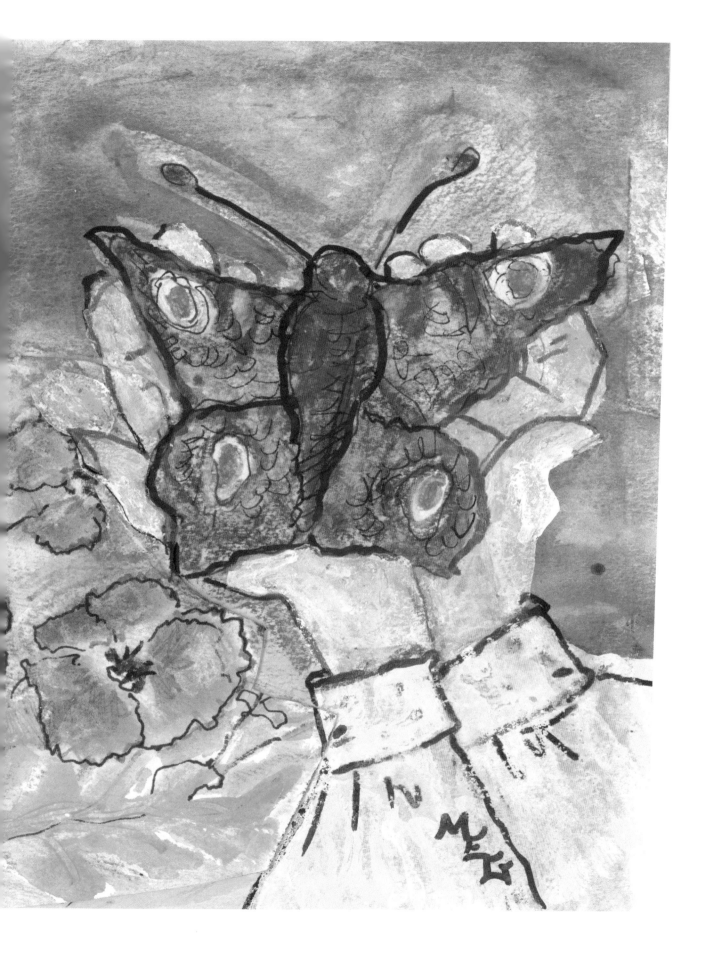

A pigeon coos, "Gene tells the life story
of a plant growing in a prison yard
to her high school, and the students
stand up and clap.
She's just like her storytelling father!"

Marmie, the cat, purrs,
"When Gene marries Mr. Porter and
moves to Geneva, Indiana, she has a
home built like one at the 1893
World's Fair. It's the cat's meow living
in Gene's gigantic 'Limberlost Cabin'!
Her bird hobby is my hobby, too!"

The Gypsy moth breezes by, "Gene brings our coccoons inside, and when we hatch, she photographs us then lets us go."

Keith Crow squawks, "Gene helps put
out a fire, asking the boy why
he uses milk instead of water.
He says the water was too hot!
The town wants to make her the
fire chief she is so fearless!"

A family of cardinals sing, "Gene buys a hat, cuts off the feathers, and writes an article about her hat shop experience!"

Gene and Mr. Porter and their daughter, Jeanette, enjoy outings to bird watch, fish, and catch turtles.

"Gene dedicates her book, 'Freckles',
to her husband, since he braves the
Limberlost Swamp with her to
observe the birth of our babies!"
cry Vern and Venus,
a pair of black vultures.

Oliver and Olivia hoot, "Gene writes over twenty books about people and animals, such as 'Girl of the Limberlost', Laddie', and 'Freckles'.
More than twenty movies are produced about her books."
The two owls fly over to land on the gates...

.....and transform into marble statues to guard 'Wildflower Woods', Gene's home, which becomes an Indiana historical museum.

Snowball and Snowflake, two
Artic Owls, toot, "Gene goes to the hills
of Hollywood to make movies and
build a new home,
'FloraAuva', in our flight path!"

A swallow swings by singing,
"Gene moves to Catalina Island
and builds another nature
homestead, 'Singing Waters'."

When Gene died in 1924, at age 61, over
500 million copies of her books
were in circulation.

Ten-thousand white pine trees were planted in her
memory at the Adirondack Forest
Preserve in New York.

Gene's wish to share her love of nature
and humanity with the world was granted by her
own hard work as a writer, painter, and
photographer.

Read her books, watch her movies,
and visit her homes turned museums.

Thought-Provoking Questions

1. Why did Gene love animals?

2. Why did animals love Gene?

3. Why did Gene cut the feathers off the hat?

4. Why did Gene help put out the fire in town?

5. Was Gene brave? How?

6. How do you know Gene's daughter liked nature?

Works Cited

Long, J. (1990). *Gene Stratton Porter: Novelist and naturalist.* Indianapolis, Indiana Historical Society.

Stratton Porter, G., (1907). *Gene Stratton Porter: A Little Story of Her Life and Work.* New York: Doubleday.

Stratton Porter, G., (1913). *Laddie: A True Blue Story.* New York: Doubleday.

Meg Ellen Grandfield taught school for
thirty years, and she teaches at two universities.
She lives on a lake in Indiana with her family.
Her desire is to inspire others to enjoy nature,
and to see life as an adventure!

If you enjoyed this book, try the other boks in
the Tabbie Tale Series by Meg Ellen Grandfield:

How the Wellwood Cat Came to Be,

Jeb Joins the Circus, and

Captain Jeb, Pirate Cat.

Made in the USA
Charleston, SC
30 June 2012